Potty Training In 3 Days

Quick And Easy Guide To Potty Training Your Toddler In As Short As 3 Days

B. Thompson

Contents

Introduction

I want to thank you and congratulate you for downloading the book, *"Potty Training In 3 Days: Quick and Easy Guide to Potty Training Your Toddler In As Short As 3 days"*.

Potty Training isn't the easiest thing in the world. Sometimes, it can make people lose patience, and that's hard when you know you have a child to rear.

However, you don't have to berate yourself or anything because there is a way for you to help potty train your child and it starts right now.

This book contains proven steps and strategies on how to potty train your child from the signs that say he's ready to be potty-trained, to what you should do, how to make sure your strategies work, potty training myths, and more.

I am a mother of three, and I remember not having a notion of where to start with this. I felt silly even asking someone as I felt like it was something that seemed obvious and that it was something I should know. I struggled with my first child. By the time my second child was ready to be potty trained, I decided to read up on the topic and try to prepare myself a lot better. However, I did think some of the information could have been improved upon and a lot of the time it seemed rather forceful. I began working as a childminder then, and I slowly homed my skills over the years. When my third child came along, I was competent in this area, and it took us only three days to train him. I must stress that every child is different, however, and they all have different learning curves, so patience is a virtue in this process.□ Thanks again for getting this book, I hope you enjoy it.

Chapter 1: Signs that Your Child Is Ready for Potty Training

First of all, you have to check if your child is ready to be potty-trained or not. Why? Well, because if a child is not ready, no matter what you do, you wouldn't be able to train Them.

So, which signs are you supposed to see, then? Here's what you have to keep in mind:

1) Is the child already able to stay dry for at least 2 hours or longer during the day?☐

2) Does your child already know how to follow basic directions? Or do they know how to imitate you when you tell them to do or say something?

3) Is your child eager to please, and wants to be praised?

4) Do they now seem interested in the potty chair? What about the toilet or the bathroom?

5) Do they now seem interested in wearing underwear?

6) Do they now complain about diapers that are dry or wet? Do they know the differences between the two?

7) Can they run and walk now?

8) Do they like things to be in their proper places?

9) Do they now try to dress themselves? ☐

10) Do they now know that they want to pee or poop by telling you through facial expressions or words?

11) Is your child now able to sit, and then rise from a potty chair?

12) Do they know how to pull their pants down, and put them up again?

13) Are they familiar with potty lingo, such as *wet, dry, pee, poop, bowel, bottom, clean,* or *messy/dirty*

If your answer to a lot of these is "yes", then chances are, your child is ready to be potty-trained. And if they are, proceed to the next chapter so you'll know what needs to be done.

Chapter 2: What You Need to Do

Now that your child is ready to be potty-trained, let us talk about how to do it.

Start with a Positive Attitude

More than anything, you need to have a positive attitude as this will show your child that the activity is fun, and it's not something they should be scared of. Once they get to keep that in mind, you'll be sure that the process will be more smooth-sailing as compared to when you act like you want to scare your child.

Prepare the Equipment...and Use a Doll!

Put the potty chair in the bathroom, or if that's still too slippery, you can try placing it in one corner of the room first. It might also be helpful if you let the child decorate the equipment, or if you can first show them how to use the equipment by making use of a doll. You see, dolls often make kids feel like they are not alone, and when you use a doll as a way to teach a child what they should do, they will easily learn things.

For example, bring the doll to the potty chair and let it sit down. Make potty noises, and then help the doll down, and say "good job", or maybe even give the doll a "star", or any form of praise. When the child sees this, they'll realize that "oh, *this is what I should do*" so the next time they feel that they want to go potty, they'll know that it's okay and that it should be done on the potty chair.

As you do this, you can also put up a "success chart" on the wall. Every time your child successfully uses the potty seat, go ahead and add fun stickers or stars and give them copies of it so they'll know they're doing something good. Positive reinforcement seriously goes a long way.

Where to begin

When first beginning, it's best to choose an entire day when you are free. I know this can be difficult for some parents, but it speeds up the learning curve. Your child will also need your undivided attention on this day, so really try your best to make sure everything is taken care of. □

Tell your child something along the lines of "Today we are going to learn to go potty like a big boy." It also helps if you say this as if it's something very exciting, that the child will enjoy. Your child will be naked or bottomless for the entire day. You are then going to spend the day trying to catch your child when they are peeing and get them to the potty during this. Makes sure the potty is close by at all times and try to move fast when getting them to the potty but not too fast because this may be frightening to the child. It also speeds up and helps the process to keep your child hydrated throughout this day. You should aim for slightly more fluid than usual but don't overdo it.

I must stress it is important that you keep a strong focus on your child throughout the day as you will want to catch them peeing as soon as you can. To pass the time I recommend playing games with them, reading books and other pass times. It is a stressful time for both of you, and it helps to get some quality time with them.☐

When the child starts peeing, try not to overreact. Simply tell your child to "Hold it in," said in a calm tone and put them on the potty immediately. Once they have gone, try and reinforce this new behavior with a reward of praise. You can say something along the lines of "Wow, well done." A lot of methods start off with you placing your child on the potty multiple times a day. However, I believe my way, at least for the first day, is more effective. I believe it helps the child associate the potty with peeing and pooping much better.

Throughout the day, you will notice your child give a funny look or behave in a certain way before they pee. As the training continues throughout the day, you will notice your child start to realize this happens earlier and earlier before the child pees. They are starting to make a connection in their brains between the feeling and the action of going to the potty. ☐

For boys, when they are on the potty, hold their penis down and teach him to do this himself.

Teaching the child to poop

You should wait until you notice a concentrated look, some grunting or any sign of discomfort. Then simply sit the child on the potty and encourage them, tell them that they can do it. Try not to be forceful or commanding as this may make it more difficult. It is best to give gentle encouragement and guidance. If your child starts crying, just try to be supportive and try your best to comfort them.☐

Praise your child if they are successful and let them know that they have done well. If you miss the kid pooping on the first day make sure to tell them "Poop goes in the potty," in a stern enough tone that they will get the message. However once again it is best not to be overly critical of them.☐

Napping

During this first day, it is important to use diapers for naps and at night time. Naps are also important for keeping your child in a mood in which they will be willing to learn, instead of cranky. ☐

Day 2

On day two we are going to schedule potty breaks throughout the day, and we are still ready to deal with them if they happen outside of these scheduled times. On this day we are going to have them wearing clothes. Something to note here is to make sure the pants are easy to get off. I also suggest starting the child with going commando for at least the next week. I believe the child is a lot more likely to catch themselves on a lot faster this way as it is a lot more of an uncomfortable feeling for them as well as a significantly different feeling than wearing diapers. ☐

So schedule times throughout the day for them to go to the potty preferably after meals when they are more likely to go. You may already know a time when your child regularly does their business if this is the case; then take them to the potty and take their diaper off. It is important to keep your child amused at this stage, so make sure you to bring a toy or a book. When you are just starting off, if they haven't yet pooped at the end of your scheduled session, simply put their diaper back on and carry on as usual until the next scheduled practice that day. □

Day 3

Again do not take it badly if on the third day if your child hasn't caught on and beginning to judge for themselves. Every child learns at different rates. It is important at this stage to let go of any judgment as it doesn't do anyone any good. On day 3 and beyond we are going to continue as previous with our scheduled times throughout the day. Try to promote your child to tell you if they need to go by emphasizing how well they are doing when they do manage to tell you. Your child will eventually get to the stage of telling you, don't worry.

How to deal with NO.

Eventually, you may be met with a strong no when you ask your toddler to go to the potty. It is important that you do not make this a battle of wills. This will be counterproductive, instead, respect their decision. Do not get upset if they then have an accident, simply reinforce that they should go to the potty to pee. It's also important you do not comfort them and tell them it is all right after they have had an accident as this could reinforce the behavior as your toddler doesn't understand the subtlety's of language yet. □

Teach the Child How to Clean

Part of potty training a child is helping him learn how to clean up too, especially with girls.

What you have to do is tell her that she should carefully wipe herself from the front all the way to the back so that germs would not fester her body and so she will also know what's hygienic and what isn't.

Teach the child how to flush their business, show them how it's done on the toilet. Once they learn how to do it, they'll be more responsible when it comes to cleaning up, or cleaning after what they've done. Of course, do not forget to tell the child to wash his or her hands afterward. Again, proper hygiene is very important.

Some Rewards and Incentives During Training

Give them a book or a toy

It will also be quite helpful if you give your child a toy or a potty-training related book for kids (*Once Upon a Potty, I Want My Potty, Sam's Potty*) so that potty training will be a fun and engaging learning experience for him.

At first, you do have to stay with your child while they're at their potty place, just to make sure that they're using the potty seat properly, and that they're not uncomfortable. Eventually, they'll learn to tell you to stay away, and that they know what needs to be done already, but it's important that you stay with them at first for proper support.

Let's say your child did not successfully potty after all if you fix a schedule for him, chances are, they might not always want to urinate or go potty, so you still have to praise him for trying to sit there and listen to you. □

If you go on vacation, it is important to bring the potty seat or check if the place has a child-friendly toilet seat, so you can continue practicing. It is important to be consistent at this phase in your child's life.

Other Incentives

Here's a list of other incentives that you can use:

1. **Coloring Books**. Help the child become more artistic by letting them work on a coloring book after each potty training session. Let them choose the book they want to use so that they will be interested.□

2. **Buy a Drink-and-Wet Doll!** You may think it's icky, but what better way to teach a child how to potty—and buy her a new toy, too—than by using a doll, specifically the *Drink-and-Wet Doll!* What this doll does is that you get to feed it or let it drink, and then she pees after. Bring her to the potty seat and your child will surely realize what needs to be done and have fun at it, too.

3. **Help them Decorate a Door Hanger**. Color it, add stickers, let them write, etc. What matters is that they'll have something to hang on the door when they feel like they have to go potty. Once they have something like this, they will be more than willing to potty because they'll be excited to use what they had made earlier.

4. **Make a Lollipop Tree.** This is just a makeshift tree made from lollipops. Give one to your child after each potty session

and chances are, they will look forward to those sessions more.

5. **Make a Happy Jar.** On popsicle sticks, write about fun things you can do in a day, or maybe during the weekend. For example, *see Frozen again, go to a theme park, make pizza,* etc. Put them in a large glass jar and have your kid pick one after each potty session. Surprises often make kids happy, and this one will surely help him learn and be happy at the same time.

6. **A Toy "Vending" Machine.** Buy one of those toy vending machines that have little toys inside them, and let your child get one after each potty session.

7. **Make a level jar.** Put some labels outside the jar. The one on the lowest would be for the first few days of potty training, and the one on top will be the best reward. Let your child add two marbles after each successful potty training session, and they'll be interested in learning—because they'll realize that in a few weeks' time, they will get something really good.

When you have the right incentives, potty training would be so much better.

Make Sure to Go Potty Fast

Now, when you see signs that your child wants to go potty or use the toilet, even if it's not on the schedule, go and bring them to their potty place right away. Take note that if they feel the need to urinate or potty, and it is out of schedule, you don't have to get mad or scold them. In fact, you should go ahead and praise them because they're telling you or showing you that they want to urinate or potty, that is already an improvement on itself, instead of them using diapers all the time.

At night, it would be best to bring them to their potty place before going to sleep so bedwetting could be avoided especially if they're already wearing underpants. If they want to pee at night, tell them to wake you up and please be patient to help them out.

Say Goodbye to Diapers, but Training Pants Are Still Okay

If weeks have already gone by, and you see that your child is slowly learning how to go potty on their own, it's probably time to say goodbye to diapers already because wearing them too long might just make way for rashes and would only slow down the pace of your child being potty-trained. □

Give your child underwear or training pants. After doing so, give them a special gift, or take them out, just make sure it is enough for them to realize that the loss of the diapers is a good thing, and is something to be celebrated. I do not recommend using training pants at the start of training as they are too much like diapers.

Now that they're using underpants, it will be fun if you let the child choose the style or color he wants. Make sure to avoid using leotards or belts, or anything that can make the act of undressing hard.

It does seem tricky at first, but just like your child, you will also get the hang of potty-training in time.

Chapter 3: How to Keep Your Potty Training Methods Working

Of course, when you potty train a child, you don't just stop when you feel like they've learned it all. There are certain things you have to do to make sure that as with anything else in life, you get to follow through.

Think of it this way: suppose you were taught a lesson today, would it just be embedded in your mind right away? Well, unless you have extremely good memory, or are interested in the subject, it might. However, it does not always happen that way for other people. In short, you have to review what you have learned for you to understand it. □

So, when it comes to potty training, you have to make sure that you do the following:

Be Patient—Even When the Child Says They Don't Want to Go Potty

Well, maybe he just does not want to go yet. Or maybe, he's shy or doesn't know what to do.

Yes, this can be frustrating, especially because you know you're just trying to do the right thing. But, you might just terrify or traumatize the child if you go and get mad at them because they do not want to go potty.

Take a Laidback Approach

Again, your child will learn better when they feel like potty training is a fun experience and that it's not something they should be scared of. When you become so angry or so strict, chances are, your child will feel like potty training is scary or that they are being reprimanded, that's not the kind of thing you want to foster.

The key here is to realize that a child learns via positive reinforcement and not by being reprimanded.

Clap Your Hands, Laugh—Keep a Lively Atmosphere During Each Session

You have to remember that kids are naturally playful. Even if it takes them some tries to get it, you have to realize that they're trying and that in itself is already a good thing because he is not repulsive. □

The very second your child gets on the potty seat, go ahead and praise them. This is already an achievement. When the child feels that they're being encouraged early on, they'd feel better, and would be more confident about themselves. Be the kind of parent who's willing to lead and encourage him every step of the way, not the kind of parent who just criticizes and scolds all the time.

Realize That He Might not Learn Everything RIGHT AWAY

Again, things like these always take time. They don't just happen right off the bat, or just because you've taught your child how to be potty-trained today doesn't mean they'll already be an expert tomorrow.

Stop thinking that there is something wrong with your child just because they do not "get" things right away. Maybe, they just need more time, and eventually, they'll learn. Do not frustrate yourself and your child by being too demanding, it never really helps anyone out.

Respect Your Child's Learning Curve

Children have different learning curves. Some learn easily, but others simply don't, but that does not mean they're not perfect or there's something wrong or terrible with them. Albert Einstein didn't speak until he was four years old, people learn at different rates, and we shouldn't judge.

When you start comparing your child to others, you're also beginning to start a painful relationship between you two. Cut it out, be patient, and know that your child will learn eventually. Put yourself in their shoes and learn to be mindful of this phase in his life.

And, Be Consistent

Consistency is the key to the success of almost everything. If you want to train your child, know that you have to be consistent, do it on schedule, and chances are, they'll pick it up faster than you think.

Once you keep this in mind, you'll make things easier for both of you.

Pulls-Ups or Underwear

This depends on the child, either or, can work however you should address this issue concerning your child's personality and their experience so far with potty training. For example, if certain children are provided with pull ups, they might be inclined to stay and keep playing after accidents happen. Whereas other children have a sense of self-pride when they go to the potty and when they feel an accident coming, they will rush to the potty. I do not recommend letting them wear pull ups during the first couple of weeks of potty training, however, as it will take away some of the child's drive to make it to the potty.□

It is also useful to test your child in different environments as they might be potty trained at home but when you take them somewhere else, this could be entirely different for them. So it's a process of trial and error from this stage. If possible prepare for the worst, I would recommend using pull ups for a little while after your child has been trained, particularly when you leave the house. □

If you want to introduce underwear to a child who is potty trained and maybe is put off by the inconvenience of going potty, then I would recommend switching to underwear. It will become uncomfortable for the child, and they will act out of necessity. You can also add in an extra motivation, by getting special underwear for them, for example, a pair with superheroes on them or their favorite T.V. show character.☐

Cost is also a factor as pull ups will be more expensive than regular diapers and so are preferably a very temporary solution.

Chapter 4: Signs that a Child Is Already Potty-Trained

So, how exactly would you know that your child is already potty-trained? Here's what you have to be mindful of:

They Already Know, and they Tell You if Their Underwear Are Wet

The very sign that a child is already potty-trained or is getting there is if they know they have wet their underwear. See, this is a sign that they're already hygienic, and they know that they have to go somewhere to pee or poop, and not just in their underwear.

They're Eager to Get Their Rewards

Why? Because they know that what they're doing is something good, and they want to prove that they are learning.

When a child learns the ideas of rewards and positive reinforcement, they begin to have that healthy competitive streak in them, and this is something good because it shows that they're understanding what you're trying to teach them. They know they will get rewards if they do something good, so of course, they will work on doing that, instead of just trying to complain, or trying not to follow you.

They Go to the Potty Chair and Try especially when they feel like they want to pee or poop

Another big sign that they're learning is when they go to their chair, and try to go potty. For one, they want to please you, and then they also know that this is right. And when they try to do what's right, it means that they are learning, and you're doing something right.

They're Proud of Their New Underpants

When they want to pick new underpants, it means that he knows he's no longer a baby and because they are no longer a "baby," they will be more responsible about his pee and poop!

Chapter 5: Signs That a Potty-Training Child Needs to See a Doctor

However, there are also times when your child seems to have an extremely hard time being potty-trained because it's a sign that they probably need to be seen by a doctor already.

How do you know if your child has to visit a doctor? Keep these things in mind:

They Strain While Trying to Pee or Poop

This is a sign that there is something wrong. After all, why would someone strain when they're not in pain, or is not ashamed of anything, right?

Maybe, there are irritations that he feels on his bun, or worse, on the genital area. Do not wait for it to get worse because even if you can't see anything, there might be something hiding there, so take him to the doctor right away.

They Have not Had a Bowel Movement in Three Days

A person, especially a child has to have a bowel movement every day. Otherwise, there might be a blockage in the rectum, and that's not a good thing. It might bring infections, and those are things you don't want your child to be afflicted with. Or maybe, he ate something that's making it hard for him to poop. Either way, medical attention needs to be sought.☐

They're Still Bedwetting, and They're Already 5 years Old

This is a problem that some parents encounter with their kids. In fact, around 90% of kids wet the bed, but the problem gets worse if the child is already 5 years and above.

Sometimes, bedwetting is inherited. But other times, certain issues make bedwetting happen, and some of these are as follows:

1. **Deep Sleeping.** Some kids are deep sleepers. Why? Well, simply because their brains don't often give the signal that they need to pee.

2. **Low Anti-Diuretic Hormone.** When a child is afflicted with this, his hormones automatically tell his kidneys that he should not urinate so much, or

that the kidneys should not make a lot of urine. And thus, what happens is that the kid releases the hormones when he is asleep—and thus, bedwetting happens.

3. **Delayed Bladder Maturation**. Some kids' bladders do not mature as fast as other kids' bladders do—and their brains only communicate with their bladder while they're asleep, and that begins to be a problem.

4. **Constipation**. Sometimes, a kid wets the bed because he's constipated.

5. **Small "Functional" Bladder**. Sometimes, a kid's bladder sends signals to the brain that it's already full—even when it's not—and so, bedwetting happens.

They Have Frequent Stains on His Underwear

These might be poop that got out when it wasn't time, or he's too embarrassed to tell you so. Sometimes, it's not just bowel stains you have to be mindful of but also bleeding or signs of wounds or laceration. Do not hesitate to take him to the doctor right away.

They Know How to Use the Potty, but Still Have Wet Pants now and then☐

This happens. Sometimes, a child is already trained, but there are moments when he'd get too wet his pants maybe because he has bedwetting or embarrassment issues, and these have to be talked about before they get worse. ☐

He Pees Every 8 to 9 Hours

Even for an adult, this is not healthy. A normal person should pee every 3 to 4 hours. Otherwise, the bladder might suffer, especially if the person has a naturally small bladder.

When a child does not pee as much as he should, chances are, he'll have problems with his kidneys, and that's not what you want to happen. So, make sure you have him checked right away.

Their Pee Hurts or Burns or They Have Intermittent Pee Stream

You know what these are? These are signs that a person has Urinary Tract Infection, and that's not an easy thing to deal with. Sometimes, it causes the genitals to blow up, or the kid to suffer from rashes, and of course, embarrassment, at some point. In the long run, it might also bring enlarged prostates which may lead to prostate cancer, so it's best that you have it checked and treated by the doctor right away.

They Complain of Hurtful Bowel Movements

There are times when they may or could suffer from bowel movements that are extremely hurtful because the bowel can't get out of the rectum easily, or because there are irritations and bleeding involved. When this happens, your child may get scared of potty training—or just the act of using the potty seat, in general. Sometimes, it also happens because of the following:

Constipation, which also causes abdominal pain, and hard stools.

Anal Fissure, this is tissue that bleeds near the rectum.

Irritable Bowel Syndrome, which causes intestinal cramps, and unwarranted spasms.

Drug Allergies, or when your child's body does not easily take medications that he needs.

Panic Attacks, which cause the rectum and other passages in the body to tighten.

Gastroenteritis, which also causes diarrhea.

Lactose Intolerance, which leads to bloating and gas.

Ulcerative Colitis, which leads to diarrhea, and cramping, among others.

Inflammatory bowel diseases, which causes swelling.

Lead Poisoning, which causes sudden rectal pain.

Remember that some kids can't easily speak up about what they're feeling—and it's your job as a parent or a guardian to make them feel like they can talk to you, and you'll help them deal with what's wrong. Don't let things take a turn for the worse, and let him be seen by a doctor—stat.

Chapter 6: Potty Training Myths—Debunked!

Finally, here are some common Potty Training Myths—all debunked for you!

"If I put my baby on the potty seat when he's 1 to 1 ½ years old, he'll easily know what's up!"

Hmmm. Let's say, there's a suspicious looking bag in the room, what would you do? Or, maybe, you saw this machine that you have not seen before in the room, are you just going to pick it up right away and use it?

Perhaps, you might let your curiosity take the better of you, but come to think of it, you really wouldn't just get something that you have not used before and use it now, would you? The same goes for your child.

So, what if there's a potty seat in the room? What do you think is he supposed to do with it when he does not know what it's about? He might see it as a toy, or just a simple distraction. After all, he's too young to learn.☐

What you can do here is guide him. Help him understand what the potty seat is about. Follow the tips that were mentioned earlier. Be the guiding force that your child needs you to be.

Do not expect your child to understand what something is about when you have not guided him yet. Everything starts with you, and you know it.

"Your child's life will be ruined if you mess up his schedule for potty training."□

No. You're not going to ruin your child's life just because you have messed up his potty training schedule, or allowed him to go potty when it's past his bedtime and the like.

You know how your child's life will be ruined? It will be ruined if you choose to criticize him for every single thing that he does, or when you become hardhearted, brutal, and just the kind of parent who cannot see anything good in his child—when in reality, this child came from you, so you should actually be proud of him.

Potty training, as much as it is for your child, is a good training for you, too. It teaches you to be patient, and believe in what your child CAN do, instead of what he CANNOT do. It teaches you to be the kind of parent who's kind and welcoming, as opposed to being someone who hates his child, and hates everyone around him. Potty training is different for everyone, and you won't mess up your child's life if he makes mistakes—same as he would not mess up yours if he makes mistakes, too. Learn from the experience, and don't treat it as something terrible.

"It will just lead to arguments between my child and me."

Never think of potty training this way. Instead, think of it as a way to help you and your child bond— crucial for his growing years. Think of it as a way to show your child that you care. After all, while potty training, you can go and read books, or go and play with some toys, and have some fun with the rewards. You can color, make art, cook, or go out after. And, the thought that you're helping your child grow into the best person he can be, cannot be compared to anything else—and you'll feel good because of it.

Just like anything else in life, when you focus on the positive part of potty training, you will realize how amazing it is to feel that you were able to nurture your child—and lead him in the right way. And when you realize that, things will become easier! ☐

Conclusion

Thank you again for getting this book. I hope it was able to help you to understand how you can train your child and how to do it well.

The next step is to make sure that you follow the tips given in this book so that you'll get to potty train your child well. Be proud of your child's eagerness to learn, and his every achievement, and you will both do well.

Finally, if you enjoyed this book, then I'd like to ask you for a favor, would you be kind enough to leave a review for this book on Amazon? It'd be greatly appreciated!

Thank you and good luck.

Check Out My Other Books

B. Thompson

Parenting Toddlers: How to Deal with Misbehaving and Challenging Toddlers

Parenting Teenage Girls: Easy guide to connect with your daughter and prepare her for the outside world

Parenting Toddlers: Solving Your Toddler's Sleep Problems A Quick and Easy Guide

Self-Love: Self-Esteem, Relationships, Joy and Happiness All Fall Into Place Once You Love Yourself☐

54796378R00024

Made in the USA
Lexington, KY
28 August 2016